the Best WOULD YOU RATHER? Book

·Book·

Buster Books

Written by
Gary Panton
Illustrated by
Andrew Pinder
Edited by Susannah Bailey
Designed by Jack Clucas

First published in Great Britain in 2022 by Buster Books,
an imprint of Michael O'Mara Books Limited,
9 Lion Yard, Tremadoc Road, London SW4 7NQ

W www.mombooks.com/buster   f Buster Books   🐦 @BusterBooks   📷 @buster_books

Copyright © Buster Books 2022

A CIP catalogue record for this book is available from the British Library.

ISBN: 978-1-78055-816-5

2 4 6 8 10 9 7 5 3 1

Papers used by Buster Books are natural, recyclable products made of wood from
well-managed, FSC®-certified forests and other controlled sources. The manufacturing
processes conform to the environmental regulations of the country of origin.

Printed and bound in February 2022 by CPI Group (UK) Ltd,
108 Beddington Lane, Croydon, CR0 4YY, United Kingdom

MIX
Paper from
responsible sources
FSC® C171272
FSC
www.fsc.org

WELCOME ...

... to *The BEST Would You Rather? Book*.
It's packed with quirky questions,
challenging choices and kooky conundrums.

On some pages, you only need to choose
between two options. On others, there are
multiple head-scratchers to select from. Some
even lead you on an adventure, where aliens,
pirates and knights in shining armour await.

Some choices are gross, some are weird, some are
hilarious and some will really get you thinking.

There are just two rules:
1. You can only choose one answer each time.
2. Don't actually try doing any of the things
in this book. That would probably be
dangerous (and also ridiculous).

TREASURE HUNT

Hidden somewhere in this book is a page of **SECRET TREASURE**. To be rich beyond your wildest dreams, all you need to do is choose the right option to these special, treasure-hunt questions.

Would you rather ...

EAT A ROTTEN FISH?

Turn to page 21

Or

STINK LIKE A ROTTEN FISH?

Turn to page 27

Would you rather lick ...

A stranger's
TOE NAIL?

Your best friend's
EAR WAX?

A **SLUG'S FACE?**

A **GORILLA'S ARMPIT?**

ODD BODS

Would you rather ...

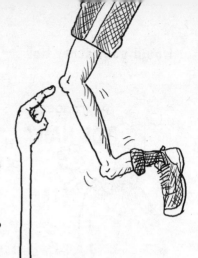

Have a second pair of knees to make your legs extra bendy?

OR

Have the world's longest arms?

Have ears the size of satellite dishes?

OR

Have a nose the length of a hot-dog?

Have a head that looks and smells like cheese, but isn't really made from cheese?

OR

Have a head that is really made from cheese, but looks and smells like a normal head?

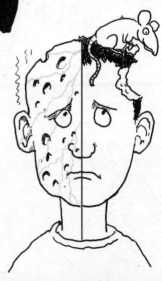

Have a foot growing out
of the top of your head?

OR

Have a head growing out
of the bottom of your foot?

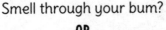

Smell through your bum?

OR

Poo through your nose?

Have fingernails that keep growing and
growing and can never be trimmed?

OR

Have tiny thumbs where each
of your fingers should be?

Have knees that bend the wrong way?

OR

Have long, straight arms with no elbows?

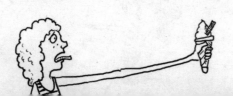

Would you rather ...
LEAD AN ARMY OF DUCKS INTO BATTLE?

Or ...
BE IN CHARGE OF ONE
GIGANTIC
WARRIOR DUCK?

AHOY! ALL ABOARD THE PIRATE GALLEON!

Arrrrr ar arrr AAAARRRRRRR arr. Arrr ha-har argh arrrrrrrrrrrGGGGGGHHHHHHHHH ar, me hearties!*

You're a pirate captain with two wooden legs and a HUGE beard. Would you rather ...

Board your old ship, *The Grumpy Skull*. She's slow, but she's scary.

Raise the Jolly Roger. It's plundering time!

Pretend you're a group of old ladies enjoying a nice cruise.

Get a new ship, *The Otter's Nose*. She's fast, but she has a silly name.

Head for Hidden Treasure Cove. You've heard there might be hidden treasure there.

Set sail for Mermaid Island. There's not much there, but you fancy a holiday.

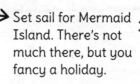

*That's pirate-speak for 'Choose your way across the seven seas.'

1. Sail up behind another ship and yell 'ARRRRR' at whoever's on board. You'll scare their scurvy socks off!

2. Follow that treasure map you've been carrying around. You'll be rich by home time!

3. Wait for another ship to invite you on board for tea and cakes, then shriek when they least suspect it.

4. Stay out of trouble all day, then when you get home tell everyone that you've been out doing some ace pirating.

5. Tell the locals you'll make them walk the plank if they don't show you where the treasure is.

6. Invite the locals back to your ship for a barbecue. Your jellyfish burgers are the best (and the wobbliest).

7. Spend all day making up silly sea shanties.

8. Spend all day teaching Squawks, your pet parrot, how to say naughty words.

What number did you end up on?
Turn the page to find out how
you did, me bucko.

Are you a perilous pirate or a no-good landlubber? Find out by checking where you ended up on the last page.

1. You're the terror of the high seas! You came top of your pirate class at Captain Crustyfeet's School for Bad 'Uns.

2. Top work – the booty is yours! No doubt you'll spend it on an even scarier beard.

3. You're a sneaky seadog, and the other pirates love you for it.

4. What a land lubber!. Hand your sea legs back and be gone!

5. Shiver me timbers, you'd make even a whale blubber.

6. You're the host with the most. It's just a pity you're supposed to be a pirate. Hang your hairy head in shame.

7. You've certainly got the musical talents of a pirate. You just need a bit less yo-ho-ho and a little more go-go-go.

8. Blow me down! You're useless at pirating, but have a future in parroting.

EXTRA PIRACY

Would you rather ...

Scrub the pirate potty?

OR

Sweep the poop deck?

Fly with the seagulls?

OR

Swim with the mermaids?

Feel sea-sick for the rest of your lily-livered days?

OR

Walk the plank?

Yell **'AVAST, YE SCURVY SQUIDS!'?**

OR

Yell **'ARRRRRRRRRRRRR, I'LL CRUSH YER BARNACLES!'?**

SUPER POWERS
Would you rather ...

Be able to leap over the tallest mountain?

OR

Be able to run faster than a cheetah?

Be able to become invisible
whenever you like?

OR

Be able to squeeze through
the tiniest spaces?

Be able to fly?

OR

Be able to breathe underwater?

Be able to tell what other people are thinking?

OR

Be able to control what other people do?

Have superhuman strength?

OR

Have X-ray vision?

Be able to transform into any animal?

OR

Be able to transform into any person?

Be able to summon fire from your fingertips?

OR

Be able to turn anything to ice?

THE PATHWAY OF **YUCK**

Can you make it all the way to the end of the dreaded Pathway of Yuck? Many have tried, but all have failed. Good luck, brave traveller.

Pick your nose and eat whatever comes out.

Pick your nose.

Start here. When you reach something you wouldn't be willing to do, you have to stop.

Carry a poo around in your pocket for a whole day.

Go for a swim in a pool full of wriggly maggots.

ANIMAL MAGIC

Would you rather ...

Camouflage like a
chameleon?

OR

Stand out like a butterfly?

Be long and thin like a weasel?

OR

Be big and dumpy like an elephant?

Be sleek and stealthy like a leopard?

OR

Be strong and muscly like a gorilla?

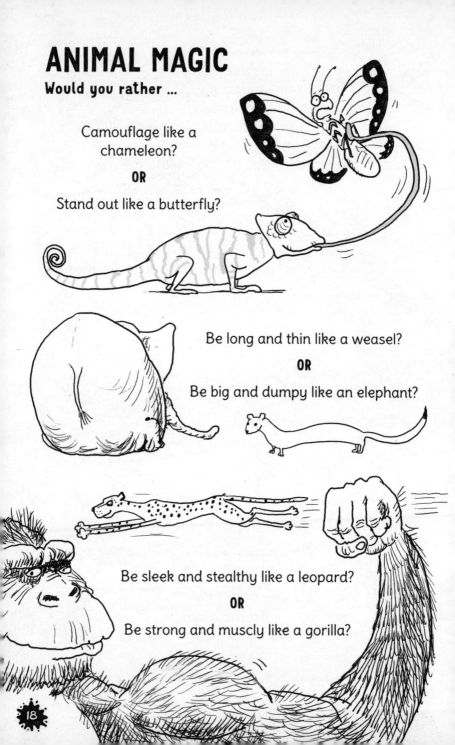

Be soggy like a sea sponge?

OR

Be slimy like a slug?

Be covered in feathers like a bird?

OR

Be covered in fur like a wombat?

Walk sideways like a crab?

OR

Slither around on your stomach like a snake?

Have a hard shell like a turtle?

OR

Wobble about like a jellyfish?

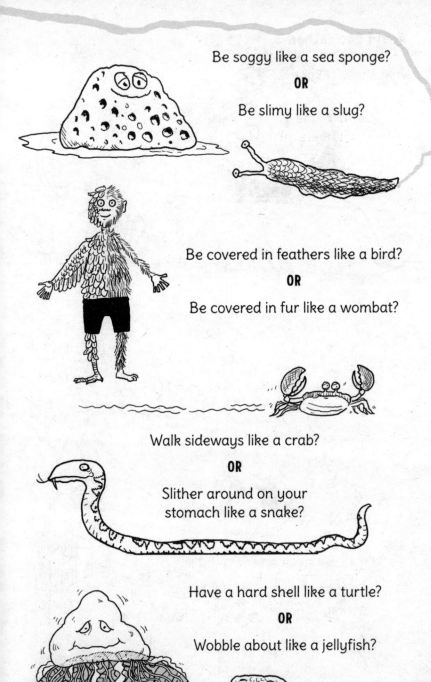

19

TREASURE HUNT

Would you rather ...

SMELL LIKE MOULDY CHEESE?

Turn to page 92

Or

SMELL LIKE WARM DUNG?

Turn to page 84

FUNKY FOOD

Would you rather eat ...

A pickled egg every day
for the rest of your life?

OR

A full jar of pickled
eggs, just once?

A million tiny sausages?

OR

One gigantic sausage that
is as big as a house?

The world's hottest chilli?

OR

A massive bowl of ice cubes?

Chocolate for the rest of your life, and nothing else?

OR

Pizza for the rest of your life, and nothing else?

A spoonful of belly-button fluff?

OR

A spoonful of snot?

Cake topped with gravy?

OR

Brussels sprouts topped with chocolate sauce?

Poo-flavoured ice cream?

OR

Ice cream-flavoured poo?

ALL GROWN UP

When you're an adult, would you rather ...

Have a job you hate,
but get paid loads
of money?

OR

Have a job you love,
but you have to
do it for free?

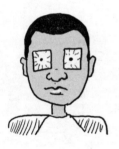

Watch every movie that
has ever been made?

OR

Play every single video game?

Live in a shack in a
beautiful tropical paradise?

OR

Live in a huge house
in the middle of a
stinky swamp?

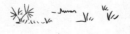

Spend every single day
in a different place?

OR

Have an amazing home
that you're never
allowed to leave?

Be ruler of your country?

OR

Win the lottery?

Be super-talented,
but no one knows
who you are?

OR

Be famous, but for
doing nothing?

Live on your own in a tent?

OR

Live in a castle with
500 other people?

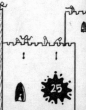

TREASURE HUNT

Would you rather have ...

HANDS FOR FEET?

Turn to page 37

Or

FEET FOR HANDS?

Turn to page 67

TECH TERROR

Would you rather ...

Get trapped forever inside your favourite video game?

OR

Get trapped forever inside your favourite TV show?

Only be able to communicate by emojis?

OR

Only be able to communicate by hand-written letters?

Always have to share a phone with your parents?

OR

Only have a phone one day a week?

Go for a week without electricity?

OR

Go for a week without running water?

Live without Wi-Fi?

OR

Live without clothes?

See everything pixelated?

OR

See everything in black and white?

Have 10 million YouTube subscribers?

OR

Make one video that gets 100 million views?

Would you rather be ...

A GIANT who

lives in a pongy sewer?

Or ...

A flea who lives in a

SMELLY ARMPIT?

MWAH-HA-HA-HA-HA!
STEP INSIDE ...
THE HAUNTED HOUSE

**Creaking floorboards. Dusty cobwebs.
A bat looking in at you through a window!
You are now entering YOUR WORST NIGHTMARE.**

You arrive at 13 Phantom Mansions, the world's most haunted house. Would you rather ...

→ Push the door open and sneak inside. You've always wanted to see a ghost!

→ Head upstairs to the attic, where you're guaranteed ghost action.

Explore the infamous BATHROOM OF TERROR.

Ring the doorbell and wait politely for someone to invite you in.

Head inside for a guided tour with Bones, the skeleton butler.

Decide that this is all too scary and stay in the garden (which is also a graveyard).

1. A GHOST COMES FLYING AT YOU. Shriek your loudest shriek, and run home as fast as you can.

2. A GHOST COMES FLYING AT YOU. Try to trick it into thinking it's you who's the ghost, by saying 'BOO' at it.

3. There's a vampire using the loo! It's a good job you're in a bathroom, because you're about to wee in terror.

4. There's a vampire using the loo! Ask it if you can have a selfie together.

5. Strike up a friendship with Bones and arrange to go on a nice holiday together later in the year.

6. Tell Bones you refuse to leave until he shows you his best ghost.

7. Look around the gravestones and make some notes. This might come in handy in history class.

8. Sit underneath a creepy old tree and rock slowly back and forth while weeping.

What number did you end up on?
Turn the page to find out how you did ... if you dare!

Are you a gutsy ghost hunter or a snivelling scaredy-cat?
Find out by checking where you ended up on the last page.

1. You were doing so well. If only you hadn't screamed like a tiny baby right at the end, there.

2. You're smarter than the average spook. You'll probably have a skeleton butler of your own one day.

3. Don't worry about how you did. Your priority is fresh pants.

4. You've no time for getting scared. You're all about getting those likes.

5. You're a kind soul, even when confronted by actual souls.

6. You sure are persistent, but the ghosts would really like for you to leave now.

7. You like to bury yourself in books (just as long as they're not too scary).

8. Let's never speak of this again.

EXTRA GHOULISHNESS
Would you rather ...

Haunt your best friend?

OR

Haunt your teacher?

Turn into a vampire bat?

OR

Turn into a werewolf?

Spend a night in a haunted house?

OR

Spend a night in a cursed graveyard?

CACKLE like a witch?

OR

WAIL like a banshee?

(Why not try out both of these options now,
to see which one you prefer?)

35

Would you rather ...

Burrow right through
the Earth and pop out
on the other side?

OR

Catapult yourself
to the Moon?

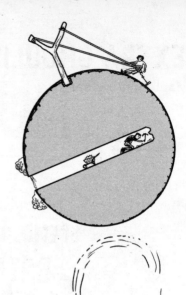

Walk across the Sahara desert
while wearing all your clothes?

OR

Walk across the South Pole
in shorts and a T-shirt?

Trampoline up to the very
highest cloud in the sky?

OR

Swim to the deepest point
of the deepest ocean?

TREASURE HUNT

Would you rather ...

SPEND AN HOUR EATING COLD PORRIDGE?

Turn to page 112

Or

SPEND AN HOUR IN A BATHTUB FILLED WITH COLD SOUP?

Turn to page 49

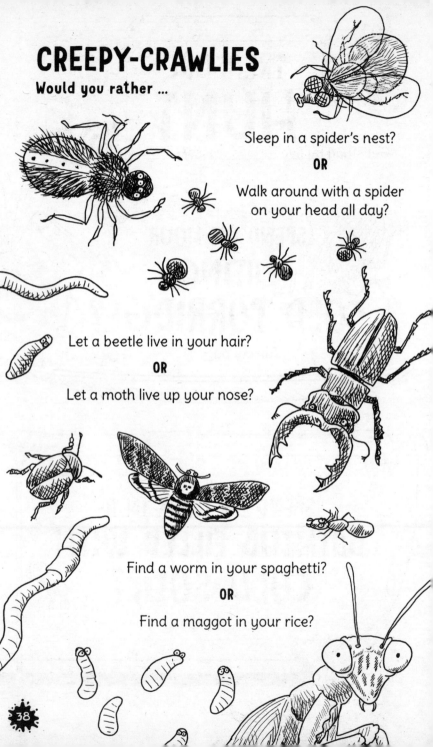

CREEPY-CRAWLIES

Would you rather ...

Sleep in a spider's nest?

OR

Walk around with a spider on your head all day?

Let a beetle live in your hair?

OR

Let a moth live up your nose?

Find a worm in your spaghetti?

OR

Find a maggot in your rice?

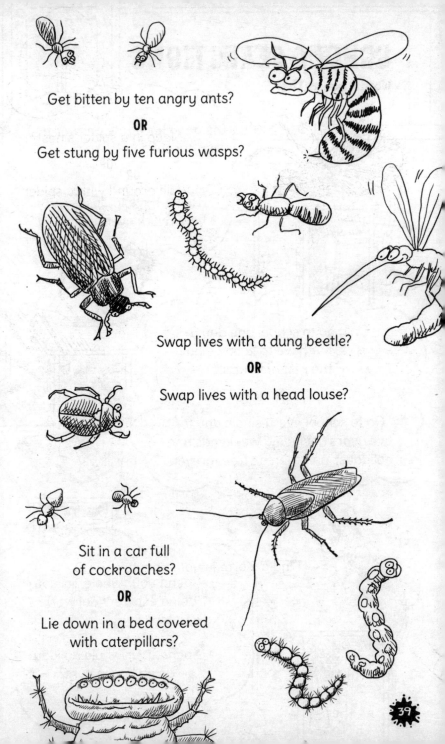

Get bitten by ten angry ants?

OR

Get stung by five furious wasps?

Swap lives with a dung beetle?

OR

Swap lives with a head louse?

Sit in a car full
of cockroaches?

OR

Lie down in a bed covered
with caterpillars?

Would you rather have ...
A HUMAN'S UPPER BODY WITH A
FISH'S TAIL?

Or ...
A FISH'S UPPER BODY WITH A
HUMAN'S LEGS?

SICK AS A PIG

Would you rather ...

Throw up every time
you see your teacher?

OR

Break out in an itchy rash every
time you see your friends?

Get the hiccups
every time you
go outside?

OR

Let out a gigantic
fart every time
you head indoors?

Have the sniffles for
the rest of your life?

OR

Have a bright-green
face for six months?

Have an allergy to laughing?

OR

Have an allergy to sitting down?

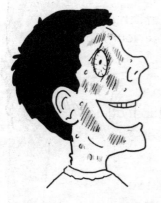

Sprout thick fur all over
your face and body?

OR

Grow scales all over
your arms and legs?

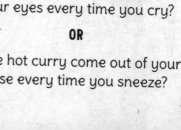

Have sticky jam come out of
your eyes every time you cry?

OR

Have hot curry come out of your
nose every time you sneeze?

WHAT NOT TO WEAR

Would you rather ...

Wear all your clothes
back-to-front?

OR

Wear all your clothes inside-out?

Wear a baseball cap that
says "I smell of bums"?

OR

Wear a T-shirt that says
"I need a cuddle-wuddle
from my teddykins"?

Wear a suit made
of cabbage leaves?

OR

Wear two hollowed-out
pumpkins for shoes?

Go to school in your pyjamas?

OR

Go out shopping in a potato sack?

Wear shoes two sizes too small?

OR

Wear shoes five sizes too big?

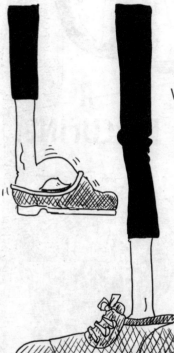

Dress up as a Halloween vampire on Christmas Day?

OR

Wear a Santa Claus costume in the middle of July?

Permanently swap all your clothes with an 80-year-old?

OR

Have to clank around in a suit of armour for a year?

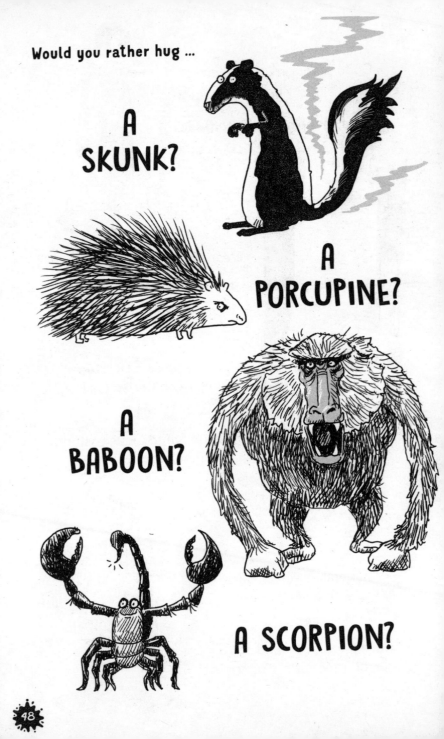

Would you rather hug ...

A SKUNK?

A PORCUPINE?

A BABOON?

A SCORPION?

TREASURE HUNT

Would you rather be ...

AS FLAT AS A PANCAKE?

Turn to page 21

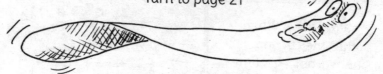

Or

AS ROUND AS A FOOTBALL?

Turn to page 67

HIGHWAY TO SMELL

Close your car windows, stick a peg on your nose and take a drive along the world's stinkiest road.

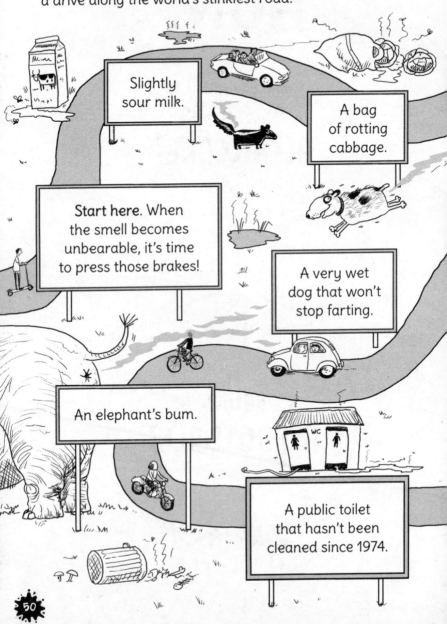

Slightly sour milk.

A bag of rotting cabbage.

Start here. When the smell becomes unbearable, it's time to press those brakes!

A very wet dog that won't stop farting.

An elephant's bum.

A public toilet that hasn't been cleaned since 1974.

Bin juice.

A very wet dog.

You made it! You should now declare yourself the Prince or Princess of Pong.

Pickled whale puke.

51

FIVE! FOUR! THREE! TWO! ONE!

BLAST OFF INTO ...

DEEP SPACE

Set your rocket engines to THHHHHRRRRRRPPPPPP!
It's time to venture into the cosmos.

You are voyaging through space in your ship, *Starmadillo II*. Would you rather ...

Head for that distant planet on your monitor. You're a space pioneer!

Land in the middle of an alien city. You like to make a dramatic entrance.

Land in a remote desert and head towards the alien city on foot.

Stay right where you are. Being on a spaceship is awesome enough!

Make yourself useful by doing some deep-space chores.

Hang out with Beep Bloop, your robot sidekick.

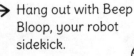

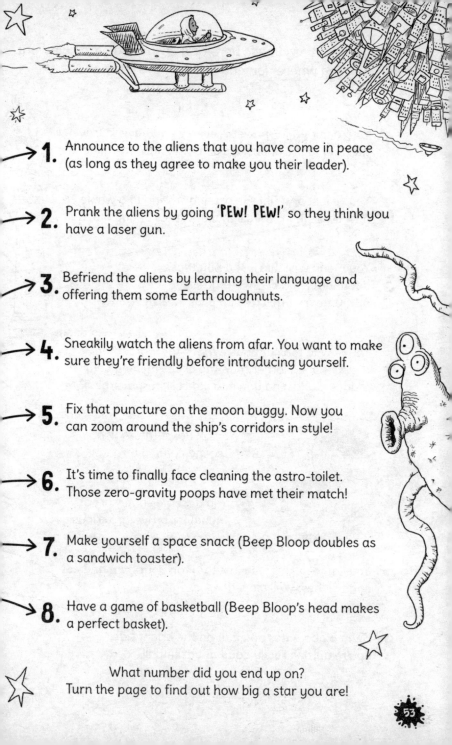

1. Announce to the aliens that you have come in peace (as long as they agree to make you their leader).

2. Prank the aliens by going 'PEW! PEW!' so they think you have a laser gun.

3. Befriend the aliens by learning their language and offering them some Earth doughnuts.

4. Sneakily watch the aliens from afar. You want to make sure they're friendly before introducing yourself.

5. Fix that puncture on the moon buggy. Now you can zoom around the ship's corridors in style!

6. It's time to finally face cleaning the astro-toilet. Those zero-gravity poops have met their match!

7. Make yourself a space snack (Beep Bloop doubles as a sandwich toaster).

8. Have a game of basketball (Beep Bloop's head makes a perfect basket).

What number did you end up on?
Turn the page to find out how big a star you are!

Are you an intergalactic hero or a cosmic coward? Find out by checking where you ended up on the last page.

1. You're thirsty for power – even if you have to travel all the way to the opposite side of the universe to get it.

2. You've just brought the art of pranking to a whole new civilization. They'll make statues of you one day.

3. You mean well. It's just a pity those doughnuts had been in cryo-sleep for 3,000 years. They're a bit past their best.

4. You're way too cautious. What's the worst that could happen (other than the aliens melting your insides or blasting you into a gazillion space-bits)?

5. Parp! Parp! Intergalactic legend coming through!

6. You deserve some sort of medal for bravery. Seriously.

7. You came all this way just to sit on your bum and eat sandwiches. Well played!

8. Beep Bloop hates you, but on the bright side you're getting really good at basketball.

ASTRO EXTRAS

Would you rather ...

Be visited by an alien?

OR

Visit an alien planet?

Be the first person to go to an amazing new planet, but you can never come home?

OR

Visit the Moon, but you can only stay there for 30 seconds?

Float around in zero gravity?

OR

Try on your very own spacesuit?

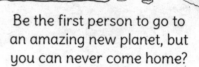

Save the world from an alien invasion?

OR

Experience life under alien rule?

55

Would you rather have the power to see ...

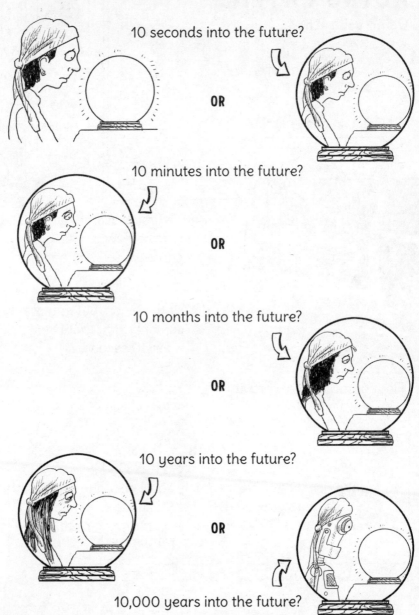

10 seconds into the future?

OR

10 minutes into the future?

OR

10 months into the future?

OR

10 years into the future?

OR

10,000 years into the future?

TREASURE HUNT

HOORAY!

At last, you've found the **SECRET TREASURE**.
You're rich! Filthy, stinking rich! You'll never have
to do a day's work in your life. Call your school
immediately and tell them you're never going back.

WHAT'S IN A NAME?

Which name would you rather be stuck with for the rest of your life?

Grotty Scotty?

OR

Barnaby Bogey?

Lady Deborah Pancake-Syrup III?

OR

Hairy Margaret?

Mick McMickmick?

OR

Poopy Plops?

Parps LaRue?

OR

Angelique Le Waaaaaaaaaah?

Purple Kenneth?

OR

Dermot Marmoset?

Fizzy Beanbags?

OR

Roly Moly?

Grumblestiltskin?

OR

Witchy Woo?

Bubbly T. Mouse?

OR

Screechy Pete?

Lord Marmaduke
Decimal-Point?

OR

Steven?

GETTING AROUND

Would you rather ...

Have to walk everywhere?

OR

Have a cool self-driving car, but it pays no attention to where you want to go?

Go to school in a horse-drawn cart?

OR

Get carried to school on someone's shoulders?

Have a teleporter that can only take you three streets away?

OR

Have a very slow rocket ship that can take you into space, but it takes 10 years to get there?

Have rollerskates that fall apart when they get wet?

OR

Have a skateboard made of beef?

Have a magical flying carpet for one week?

OR

Have a swanky sports car for the rest of your life?

Travel to the bottom of the deepest sea trench in a submarine?

OR

Fly at top speed over a mountain range in a helicopter?

Have a super-fast bike with turbo rockets on the sides?

OR

Have springy shoes that let you bounce over the tallest buildings?

61

A
KING
OR
QUEEN?

A SUPERHERO?

A FAMOUS
MOVIE STAR?

WAKEY WAKEY!

Would you rather ...

Be woken up by a massive chicken pecking at your feet?

OR

Be woken up by a blobfish sitting on your face?

Wake up as a different person every morning?

OR

Stay yourself, but you have to re-live the same day every day?

Wake up knowing the answers to every test or exam you'll ever have to sit?

OR

Wake up with a MASSIVE pile of money sitting next to your bed?

Never need to sleep again?

OR

Never need to poo again?

Have a week with no sleep?

OR

Have a week with lots of sleep but constant nightmares?

Have to go to bed and sleep every two hours (even during the day)?

OR

Have to get up and dance every two hours (even at night)?

Wake up at school in just your pants?

OR

Wake up fully clothed in a swamp, with no idea how you got there?

CHALLENGE ACCEPTED
Would you rather ...

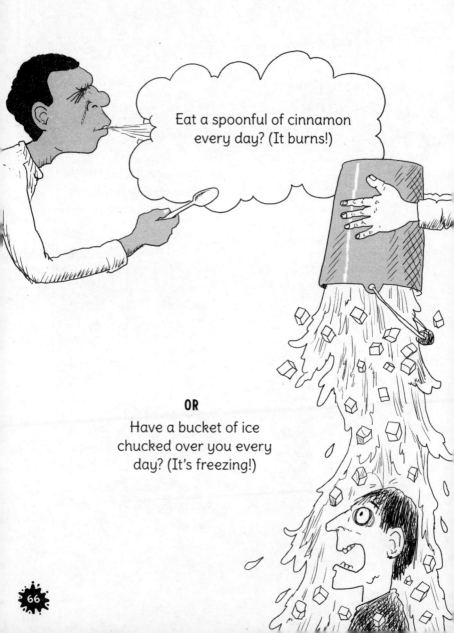

Eat a spoonful of cinnamon every day? (It burns!)

OR

Have a bucket of ice chucked over you every day? (It's freezing!)

TREASURE HUNT

Would you rather ...

HAVE A TINY HEAD ON TOP OF A MASSIVE BODY?

Turn to page 49

Or

HAVE A MASSIVE HEAD ON TOP OF A TINY BODY?

Turn to page 103

CREATURE CONUNDRUMS

Would you rather ...

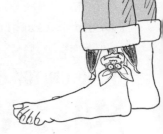

Have a bird make a
nest in your hair?

OR

Have a bat live
in your trousers?

Cuddle a snake?

OR

Kiss a toad?

Only be able to
gobble like a turkey?

OR

Only be able to
moo like a cow?

Be able to command all the bugs in the world to do your bidding?

OR

Have a chimp companion who does anything you ask?

Have a talking dog, but it's really mean and calls you nasty names all day?

OR

Have a sweet (but normal) dog who can't do any special tricks?

Discover that all the other people in the world have been turned into monkeys?

OR

Find yourself and one friend turned into monkeys, while everyone else is fine?

Would you rather always ...

BE SLEEPY?

BE
BORED?

BE
HUNGRY?

BE THIRSTY?

BE GRUMPY?

NEED A WEE?

RICH AND FAMOUS

Would you rather ...

Be a Hollywood
movie star?

OR

Be a world-famous
sports star?

Have your life story made
into a blockbuster movie?

OR

Be turned into the star
of a hit video game?

Be famous for being
an evil villain?

OR

Be a really good person,
but no one knows
who you are?

Be the world's best singer, but never be famous?

OR

Be the world's worst singer, and be famous for it?

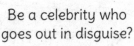

Be a celebrity who goes out in disguise?

OR

Be a celebrity who signs lots of autographs and lets fans take loads of selfies?

Have your entire life broadcast on TV?

OR

Have all your thoughts posted online?

Score the winning goal in the World Cup final?

OR

Become King or Queen and get to boss everyone else around?

NICE 'N' SPICY

Would you rather ...

Drink a jug of
vindaloo curry?

OR

Take a bath in
chilli con carne?

Brush your teeth
with chilli sauce?

OR

Gargle with hot mustard?

Keep a raw chilli pepper
up your nose all day?

OR

Eat a heaped spoonful
of horseradish?

TREASURE HUNT

Would you rather ...
EAT A MUD SANDWICH?

Turn to page 84

Or
DRINK A BOGEY MILKSHAKE?

Turn to page 57

FLUSHED AWAY

Wheee! You've just been flushed down the loo. How far can you make it through the poo pipe before you have to stop, as what you're finding is too disgusting?

Used bits of loo roll.

Someone's pants.

Start here. No matter how bad things get, try not to give up!

A lost pigeon.

A really big poo.

An even bigger poo.

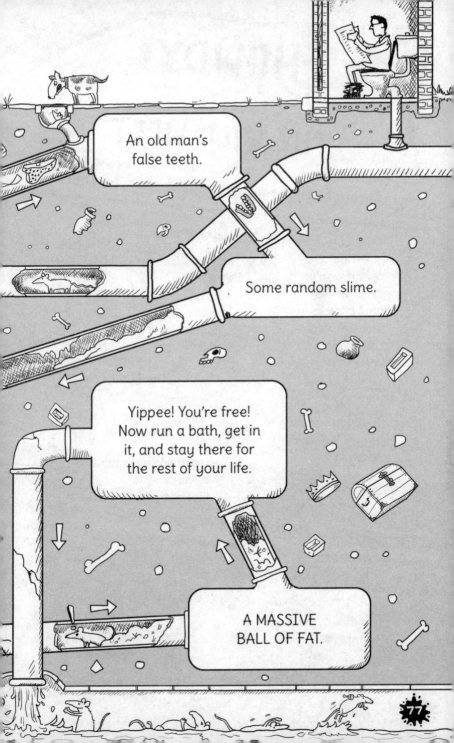

HOWDY!
WELCOME TO ...
THE WILD WEST

Yeeeeeeeeeeeeeeeeeeeeee-haw! Mosey your way through these rootin'-tootin' choices, partner!

Whether you're a cowboy or a cowgirl, you've got yourself some choices to make. Would you rather ...

Saddle up Old Betsy (your favourite horse) and head off looking for adventure.

Find some bad guys up to no good. It's time to clean up this town.

Gallop alongside a moving train for no reason. Yee-haw!

Stay at the ranch to practise your ace lasso skills.

Head on over to the biggest bull and look him square in the eye.

Pick an itty-bitty calf to start with. Even the best have to start somewhere.

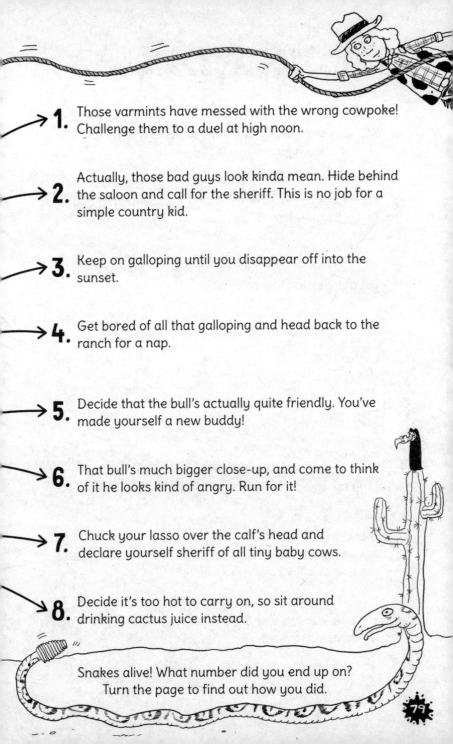

1. Those varmints have messed with the wrong cowpoke! Challenge them to a duel at high noon.

2. Actually, those bad guys look kinda mean. Hide behind the saloon and call for the sheriff. This is no job for a simple country kid.

3. Keep on galloping until you disappear off into the sunset.

4. Get bored of all that galloping and head back to the ranch for a nap.

5. Decide that the bull's actually quite friendly. You've made yourself a new buddy!

6. That bull's much bigger close-up, and come to think of it he looks kind of angry. Run for it!

7. Chuck your lasso over the calf's head and declare yourself sheriff of all tiny baby cows.

8. Decide it's too hot to carry on, so sit around drinking cactus juice instead.

Snakes alive! What number did you end up on?
Turn the page to find out how you did.

Are you a fearless hero or a silly city slicker?
Find out by checking where you ended up on the last page.

1. You sure are brave! You've saved the town and you'll be invited to every hoedown in the west.

2. You're less cow*boy* than cow*ard*. Don't worry, though. It can be your little secret.

3. You need to ride all the way back home again now, but at least you looked pretty cool.

4. Your heart's not in this wild west life, is it?

5. You sure do have a way with animals. This is your dream job!

6. A cowpoke who's scared of cattle? That could be a bit of a problem. Didn't you read the job description?

7. If there's ever a vacancy for a cowboy or cowgirl who specializes in dealing with very small baby cows, you'll be first in line.

8. Yuck! At least choose a drink that tastes nice.

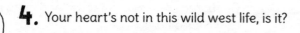

EVEN WILDER WEST

Would you rather ...

Be challenged to a duel by the meanest bank robber in town?

OR

Be challenged to spend all day clinging to a bucking bronco?

Spend a whole day sitting on a very prickly cactus?

OR

Be charged by a bull with huge horns?

Slurp down a huge sloppy bowl of lava-hot Texan chilli?

OR

Munch through a huge helping of extra-farty cowboy beans?

Change your name to

CACTUS JOE, PEST OF THE WEST?

OR

STETSON SAM, GLUTTON OF GIZZARD GULCH?

FOOD FOR THOUGHT

Would you rather ...

Eat something healthy
that tastes like sick?

OR

Eat something delicious
that will give you a
three-day tummy ache?

Sweat droplets of cold soup?

OR

Cry tears of cold gravy?

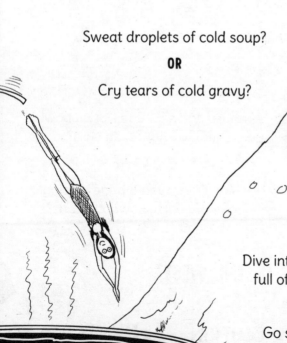

Dive into a swimming pool
full of liquid chocolate?

OR

Go sledging down a
mountain of ice cream?

Be given as much free food as you like for the rest of your life?

OR

Be able to travel anywhere you want for free for the rest of your life?

Live in a gingerbread house (but if you eat it you'll be homeless)?

OR

Live in a normal house but the floor is permanently coated in a thin layer of custard?

Have a fairly disappointing dessert after every single meal?

OR

Have the greatest dessert anyone has ever tasted, but once you've finished it you can never eat dessert ever again?

TREASURE HUNT

Would you rather ...

HAVE A VERY SQUEAKY, HIGH-PITCHED VOICE, LIKE A TINY MOUSE?

Turn to page 67

Or

HAVE A VERY DEEP, LOW-PITCHED VOICE, LIKE A BLUBBERY WHALE?

Turn to page 103

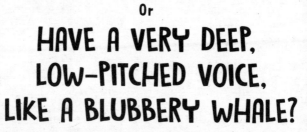

Would you rather sleep ...

IN A BEAR'S CAVE?

IN A COFFIN?

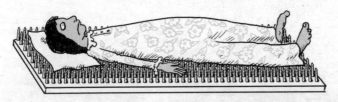

ON A BED OF NAILS?

ON THE WINGS OF AN

AEROPLANE TAKING OFF?

Or ...

Be followed around forever by

YOUR OWN PERSONAL
RAIN CLOUD?

87

WHAT WOULD YOU CALL YOUR CAT?

Mr Whiskers?

OR

Paw-naldo?

Furbert?

OR

Catilda?

Lady Pussington?

OR

Scratchy Prudence?

Terry the Tiny Tiger?

OR

Santa Claws?

WHAT WOULD YOU CALL YOUR DOG?

Sir Barksalot?

OR

Furry Dave?

Madame Puppernickel?

OR

Waggles the Wonder-Dog?

Wolfgang?

OR

M. C. Growlz?

Dogzilla?

OR

Houndsley?

GETTING HAIRY

Would you rather ...

Cough up a hairy pellet
after every meal, like an owl?

OR

Have long, silky hair growing
from your tongue?

Find a stranger's
hair in your food?

OR

Find a stranger's
food in your hair?

Wash your hair
with toilet water?

OR

Use some extra-gloopy
snot as hair gel?

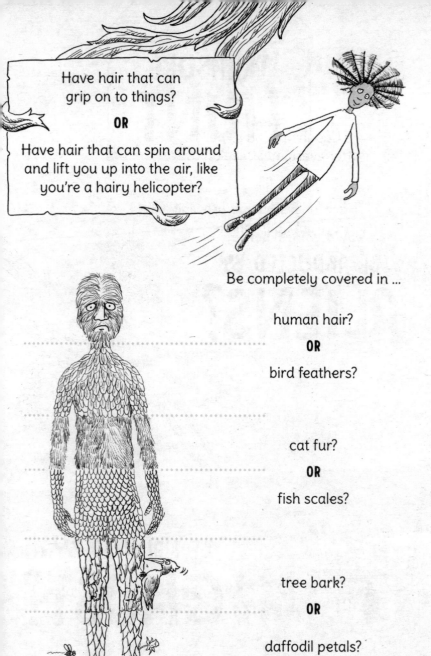

Have hair that can grip on to things?

OR

Have hair that can spin around and lift you up into the air, like you're a hairy helicopter?

Be completely covered in ...

human hair?

OR

bird feathers?

cat fur?

OR

fish scales?

tree bark?

OR

daffodil petals?

TREASURE HUNT

Would you rather ...
BE ABDUCTED BY
ALIENS?

Turn to page 84

Or
BE HAUNTED BY A
GHOST?

Turn to page 27

Would you rather ...

Be the only human who can talk to animals (but they can't talk back to you)?

OR

Be the only human who animals can talk to (but you can't talk back to them)?

You can only be ONE of these things
for the rest of your life.

WHICH ONE WILL YOU CHOOSE?

A BABY

A 90-YEAR-OLD

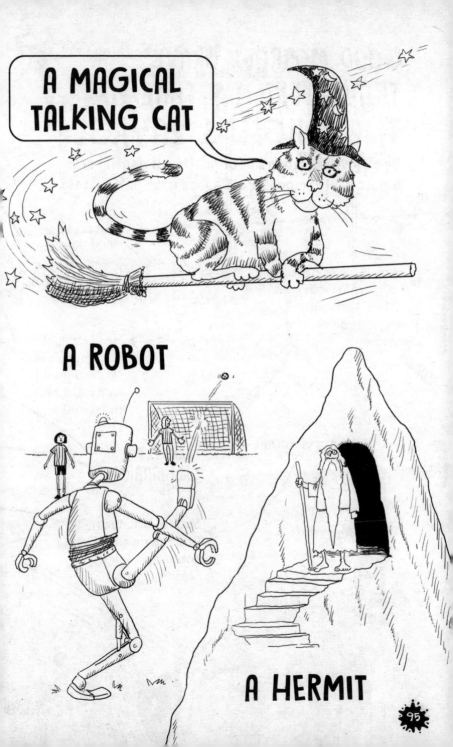

GOOD MORROW, BRAVE TRAVELLER! IT'S TIME FOR ...
THE KNIGHT'S VOYAGE

Don't just sit around your castle all day! There's heroic stuff to be done. Choose your path wisely.

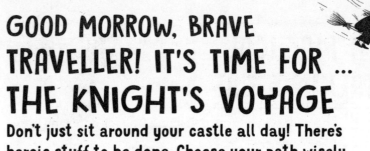

You're a brave knight, clanking around in loads of cool armour. **Would you rather ...**

Rescue your true love from the pesky dragon.

Find the Wise Witch. She can put the dragon under a sleeping spell.

Head straight for the dragon's lair. No one messes with a knight of the realm!

Save the villagers from the goblin army.

Goblins in sight: **CHAAAAARGE!**

Stroll over to the Head Goblin for a chat. Even goblins can listen to reason, right?

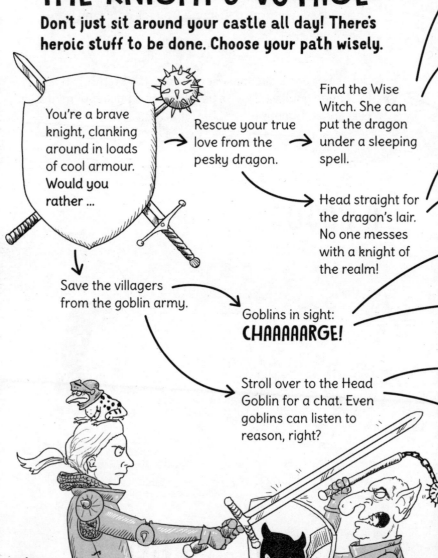

1. Speak to the witch nicely. You're in luck – she likes you! The dragon slumbers and your true love is free. No kissing, please.

2. Demand that the witch does as you say. Bad idea. The Wise Witch turns you into a frog for annoying her. Ribbit!

3. Ugh, someone's got some serious dragon breath. Exchange your true love's freedom for a packet of mints. Everyone's happy!

4. That dragon's a bit scary up close, isn't it? Maybe your true love can find their own way out. See ya!

5. Wave your massive sword around in the air and send those goblins galloping. The villagers are saved!

6. Do a U-turn when you see how well the goblins are settling into village life. Maybe everyone can just get along after all.

7. Tell the Head Goblin to leave immediately. The Head Goblin takes one look at you and whacks you over the head with his whacking stick.

8. Offer the Head Goblin some home-baked sponge cake. He's so touched that he scoffs the lot and withdraws his troops. The village is saved!

Huzzah! Your voyage is complete. What number did you end up on? Turn the page to find out how you did.

Are you a good, kind, brave, heroic knight or a rubbish one? Find out by checking where you ended up on the last page.

1. Your dashing charm won the day and everyone loves you (except for that dragon).

2. Hopefully you'll find someone willing to kiss you and turn you back into a human. Good luck with that, Froggy Face!

3. You never leave home without some mints in your pocket, and it's finally paid off.

4. Looks like you don't need any of that armour. Maybe you should wear a CHICKEN costume instead.

5. You're a true hero, and you look great with a sword. In years to come, minstrels will sing songs about your awesome adventures.

6. You're a peace-lover at heart. You maybe should have thought about that before you became a knight.

7. You're going to have a killer headache in the morning. That'll teach you not to get gutsy with a goblin.

8. It's a good thing your baking is so good. Goblins can't stand a soggy bottom.

CASTLE CONUNDRUMS

Would you rather ...

Sneak into a dragon's lair and help yourself to its treasure?

OR

Sneak into a witch's house and grab her book of spells?

Grow your hair really long so that strangers can climb up it, like Rapunzel?

OR

Spend all day snoozing, like Sleeping Beauty?

Live in a castle in medieval times?

OR

Live in a space-age house 500 years into the future?

Be a brave, heroic knight with no armour?

OR

Be a terrible knight, but have the best armour and an amazing sword?

If you could remove just ONE of these things from your life forever, which one would you pick? Choose wisely!

DOING CHORES

GOING TO SCHOOL

VISITING THE DENTIST

EATING
VEGETABLES

CATCHING
A COLD

WEARING ANYTHING
YOU DON'T
WANT TO

Would you rather be challenged to ...

 **A SNOWBALL FIGHT?**

 **A FOOD FIGHT?**

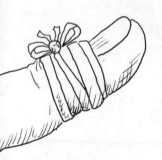 **A THUMB WAR?**

A WATER BALLOON BATTLE?

TREASURE **HUNT**

Would you rather ...
NEVER STOP
BURPING?
Turn to page 49

Or
NEVER STOP
SNEEZING?
Turn to page 21

WHAT'S THAT PONG?

Would you rather ...

Stink, but only other people can smell you?

OR

Find everyone else stinky, but only you can smell them?

Never change your socks for the rest of your life?

OR

Never wash your hair ever again?

Go for a swim in some sewage?

OR

Fall into a skip full of used nappies?

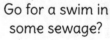

Would you rather be the world's ...

FUNNIEST PERSON?

SMARTEST PERSON?

HAPPIEST PERSON?

FRIENDLIEST PERSON?

RICHEST PERSON?

MOST TALENTED PERSON?

FASTEST PERSON?

LUCKIEST PERSON?

BIZARRE BODIES

Would you rather ...

Have a tongue so long that it dangles out of your mouth and right down to your feet?

OR

Have earlobes so long that they drag along the ground when you walk?

Have two heads that disagree on everything?

OR

Have four legs that all try to walk in different directions?

Have wheels where your feet should be?

OR

Have wings where your arms should be?

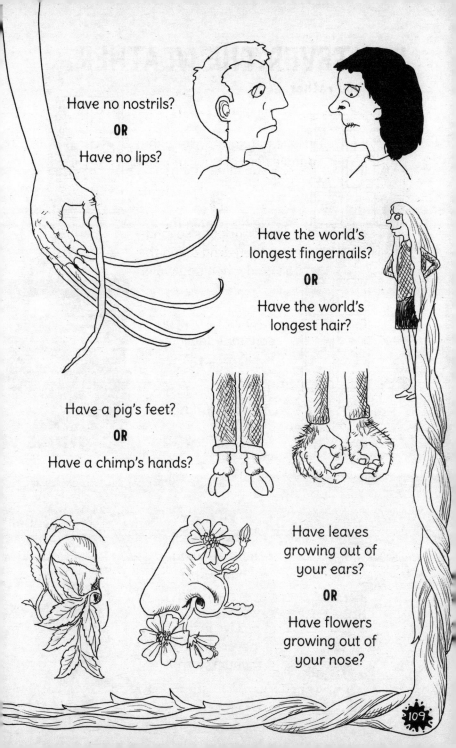

Have no nostrils?

OR

Have no lips?

Have the world's longest fingernails?

OR

Have the world's longest hair?

Have a pig's feet?

OR

Have a chimp's hands?

Have leaves growing out of your ears?

OR

Have flowers growing out of your nose?

WHATEVER THE WEATHER

Would you rather ...

Never go out in the
sunshine again?

OR

Never play in the
snow again?

Live in a world of
constant daylight?

OR

Live in a world of
constant darkness?

Live in a
never-ending
hailstorm?

OR

Live in a
never-ending
thunderstorm?

Have to walk home through
snow with no shoes or socks on?

OR

Have to run home across a
scorching desert while wearing
all your clothes at the same time?

Have the power to
summon thunder
and lightning?

OR

Have the power to
summon thick fog?

Build the world's
tallest snowman?

OR

Build the world's
biggest sandcastle?

Go outside when
it's raining frogs?*

OR

Go outside when
it's raining fish?*

*Both of these really happen!

TREASURE
HUNT

Would you rather ...

HAVE A
HUGE BEARD
WITH BITS OF FOOD
STUCK IN IT?

Turn to page 67

Or

HAVE A LONG,
STIFF MOUSTACHE
THAT BIRDS KEEP
TRYING TO PERCH ON?

Turn to page 75

Would you rather lick ...

A PUBLIC BIN?

AN OLD SHOE?

A PAVEMENT?

A DOG'S BOWL?

Would you rather ...

TRAVEL BACK TO
PREHISTORIC TIMES
AND RIDE AROUND ON A **TRICERATOPS?**

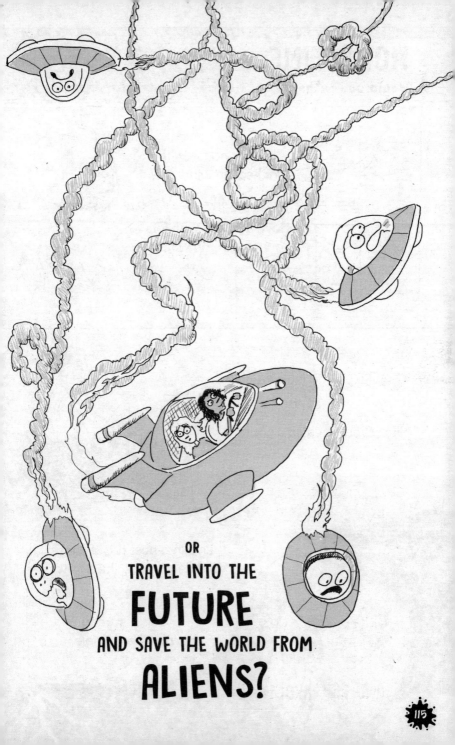

OR
TRAVEL INTO THE
FUTURE
AND SAVE THE WORLD FROM
ALIENS?

HOME TIME
Would you rather ...

Have a house with bricked-up windows?

OR

Have a house with lots of holes in the walls?

Sleep in an icy cave?

OR

Eat every meal in a sauna?

Live in a nest full of sticks and dead mice, like a hawk?

OR

Live in a muddy burrow, like a mole?

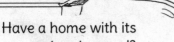

Have a home with its own swimming pool?

OR

Have a home with its own go-kart track?

Live in a country where you don't understand the language?

OR

Understand every language, but have to move to a new country every week?

Live high up on a mountain, like a goat?

OR

Live deep under the sea, like a squid?

Live in a house that is very slowly filling up with tomato ketchup?

OR

Live in a house that is very slowly getting smaller?

Would you rather have an evil wizard change you into ...

A MONKEY?

A TOAD?

A GIANT?

A TOILET?

118

TREASURE HUNT

Would you rather ...

HAVE A PERMANENTLY RUNNY NOSE?

Turn to page 67

Or

HAVE A PERMANENTLY ITCHY BUM?

Turn to page 4

You can rid the whole world of just one thing from this list. Which one will you choose?

BED TIME

BEING GROUNDED

TEACHERS

BAD SMELLS

You can keep just one of these things in the world – the rest are banned forever. Which one will you choose?

JOKES

ROLLER-COASTERS

HOLIDAYS

CAKES

WHIZZ! ZOOM! QUICKFIRE ROUND WHOOSH! PEW!

You have to answer the questions on the next six pages **INSTANTLY**. That means no pausing, hesitating or going 'ummmm'. Ready ... steady ... **GO! GO! GO!**

Would you rather ...

Eat mud?

OR

Eat someone else's bogeys?

Never change your pants?

OR

Never wash your face?

Always be hot and sweaty?

OR

Always be cold and shivery?

Wear clothes that are
two sizes too small?

OR

Wear clothes that fit perfectly
and look great, but are
permanently wet?

Have four legs?

OR

Have four arms?

Wear a teddy bear
onesie every day?

OR

Wear a ballerina
outfit every day?

Eat soup with a fork?

OR

Eat jelly with
your hands?

Don't stop here. Turn the page! ⟶

QUICKFIRE ROUND (CONTINUED)

Would you rather ...

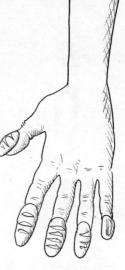

Have teeth made of wood?

OR

Have fingernails made of bread?

Have a monkey photobomb every selfie you ever take?

OR

Never appear in another photo for the rest of your life?

Spend a year completely on your own?

OR

Spend a year with one super-annoying person?

Have ears that can listen in on anything you want anywhere in the world, but they're bright blue?

OR

Have a third eye that looks out of the back of your head, but you can only use it when your other eyes are closed?

Be 30 minutes late for everything?

OR

Be an hour early for everything?

Get lost in the woods?

OR

Get lost in the roughest part of town?

Go to a party where the music's way too loud?

OR

Go to a party where the music's way too quiet?

KEEP GOING! →

QUICKFIRE ROUND (CONTINUED)

Would you rather ...

Find a magical bowl that refills itself with any food you want?

OR

Find a magical key that lets you unlock any door in the world?

Live on the top floor of the tallest skyscraper?

OR

Live on the bottom floor of the deepest underground bunker?

Go on holiday and forget to bring any underpants?

OR

Get on the wrong plane and have to go on holiday to somewhere rubbish?

Live at home with your family but
you're not allowed to talk to them?

OR

Live on the other side of the
world from your family, but
you can video-call them
whenever you like?

Be legally allowed to commit one
crime with no consequences?

OR

Never have to wait in
a queue again?

Cough up 20 ants?

OR

Sneeze out one mouse?

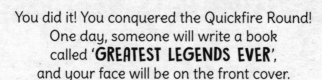

You did it! You conquered the Quickfire Round!
One day, someone will write a book
called **'GREATEST LEGENDS EVER'**,
and your face will be on the front cover.

THE LAST PAGE

Would you rather ...

Have to do all the things you've chosen in this book ... **FOR REAL?**

OR

Close this book **IMMEDIATELY** and never mention any of this to anyone ever again?

ALSO AVAILABLE:

ISBN: 978-1-78055-784-7   ISBN: 978-1-78055-708-3   ISBN: 978-1-78055-785-4

ISBN: 978-1-78055-626-0   ISBN: 978-1-78055-624-6   ISBN: 978-1-78055-625-3   ISBN: 978-1-78055-635-2